Omelettes, Frittatas & Soufflés

Omelettes, Frittatas & Soufflés

SIMPLE & INSPIRING RECIPES WITH EGGS

Susannah Blake

LORENZ BOOKS

This edition is published by Lorenz Books

Lorenz Books is an imprint of Anness Publishing Ltd
Hermes House, 88–89 Blackfriars Road, London SE1 8HA
tel. 020 7401 2077; fax 020 7633 9499
www.lorenzbooks.com; info@anness.com

This edition distributed in the UK by Aurum Press Ltd
tel. 020 7637 3225; fax 020 7580 2469

This edition distributed in the USA and Canada by National Book Network;
tel. 301 459 3366; fax 301 459 1705; www.nbnbooks.com

This edition distributed in Australia by Pan Macmillan Australia
tel. 1300 135 113; fax 1300 135 103
customer.service@macmillan.com.au

This edition distributed in New Zealand by David Bateman Ltd
tel. (09) 415 7664; fax (09) 415 8892

Publisher: Joanna Lorenz
Managing Editor: Linda Fraser
Senior Editor: Susannah Blake
Editorial Reader: Richard McGinlay
Photographers: Tim Auty, Amanda Heywood, William Lingwood, Steve Moss
  Craig Robertson
Recipes: Catherine Atkinson, Alex Barker, Yasuko Fukuoka, Nicola Graimes,
  Maggie Mayhew, Christine McFadden, Jennie Shapter
Production Controller: Claire Rae

10 9 8 7 6 5 4 3 2 1 0

NOTES
Bracketed terms are intended for American readers. For all recipes, quantities
are given in both metric and imperial measures and, where appropriate,
measures are also given in standard cups and spoons. Follow one set, but not
a mixture, because they are not interchangeable. Standard spoon and cup
measures are level.: 1 tsp = 5ml, 1 tbsp = 15ml, 1 cup = 250ml/8fl oz
Australian standard tablespoons are 20ml. Australian readers should use 3 tsp
in place of 1 tbsp for measuring small quantities of gelatine, flour, salt, etc.

Medium (US large) eggs are used unless otherwise stated.

Contents

Cooking with Eggs

Almost everyone has a supply of eggs in the refrigerator and, with a little help from this book, they also have the skill to prepare irresistible savoury and sweet omelettes and soufflés. These are among the easiest, yet most spectacular of dishes, and all you need to produce perfect results is a little know-how.

For versatility, you can't beat an omelette – although you have to beat the eggs. A simple omelette flavoured with fresh herbs or grated cheese makes a quick, tasty lunch. If you want something a little more substantial, try an Italian frittata or its even more filling cousin, the Spanish omelette. Vegetables – and other ingredients if you like – and beaten eggs are cooked in the same pan to produce a delicious flat omelette that can be cut into wedges to serve several people. It's the perfect choice for the busy cook.

Hot soufflés are scarcely any more effort, but never fail to impress. They can be filled with cheese, vegetables, fish or fruit. The golden rule is to serve them immediately they are ready – puffed up and golden brown.

The technique for making cold soufflés is slightly different but the results are just as spectacular. As you need to allow time for the mixture to set and chill, they are ideal for entertaining, because all the preparation is out of the way and you can be confident that the meal's finale will be sensational.

The secrets of success

SEPARATING EGGS

You can't make an omelette without breaking eggs and you can't make a soufflé without separating them.

1 Tap the egg firmly on the side of a bowl near to the middle of the shell. Alternatively, make an indent in the shell by tapping it with a knife blade.

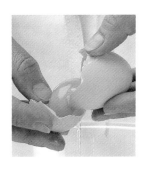

2 Holding the egg over the bowl, prise the shell apart with your thumbs without breaking pieces off. Turn the half containing the yolk upright and let the white drain into the bowl.

3 Tilt the half-shells and slip the yolk from one half to the other, without breaking the yolk. Continue to do this until all the white has drained into the bowl. Transfer the yolk to another bowl.

WHISKING EGG WHITES

It is essential that all the equipment used for whisking egg whites is completely grease-free and thoroughly dry, otherwise the egg white will not foam up. A copper bowl is said to be the best for this purpose because a chemical reaction between the egg white and the copper strengthens and stabilizes the foam. However, do not leave the whisked white standing in the bowl because, after about 15 minutes, it will turn grey. Glass and ceramic bowls also work well, but it is difficult to be sure of removing all traces of grease from plastic ones. Whatever the material, the bowl needs to be large enough to allow the egg whites to expand in volume.

Whisk the egg whites with a balloon whisk or a hand-held electric mixer until they are stiff but not dry. Adding a pinch of salt helps stabilize the whites. For sweet dishes, gently whisk the egg whites until foamy, then add the sugar, a little at a time, whisking vigorously or, with an electric mixer at a higher speed, until stiff and glossy.

CHECKING EGGS FOR FRESHNESS

The fresher the egg, the better it will taste. Suppliers provide a "use by" date and you should never ignore this. Eggs may be stored for up to one month in the refrigerator. They are best kept in a box, pointed end downwards. Using the refrigerator's egg rack exposes them to contaminating smells. Do not wash eggs, as this makes the shell even more permeable to odours. If you are planning to whisk egg whites, remove the eggs from the refrigerator 30 minutes beforehand to allow them to come to room temperature.

A fresh egg feels heavy for its size. To test for freshness, mix together 500ml/17fl oz/2¼ cups water and 60ml/4 tbsp salt, stirring until the salt has dissolved. Place the egg in the bowl of salted water. If it sinks to the bottom, it is fresh. If it positions itself halfway up, it is still edible, but no longer really fresh. If it floats on the top, it has gone bad and you would be well advised not to crack it open.

BROWN OR WHITE?

There is no truth to the myth that brown eggs are in some way healthier than white. They both have the same nutritional contents. The colour of the yolk, which can range from pale yellow to deep gold, is no indicator of quality or freshness either.

Cook's Tip

If there are any traces of yolk in the egg whites, you will not be able to whisk them properly. Drain each egg white into a separate bowl and then combine, so that if you have an accident with the yolk of one, it doesn't ruin all the others.

Making Omelettes

Although special omelette pans are available, any heavy, medium-size, non-stick frying pan will do. Prepare flavourings and fillings first and have a warm serving plate ready. Do not start to cook until you are ready to eat, as an omelette can take as little as three minutes from start to finish.

Basic omelette

Traditionally rolled or folded to enclose a filling, an omelette can also be served flat and topped with any flavouring ingredients.

1 Allow 3 eggs per omelette and break them into a bowl. Add salt, pepper and any other seasonings and lightly beat with a fork.

2 Melt 15g/½oz/1 tbsp butter in an omelette pan or frying pan. When it is sizzling, but not smoking or browning, pour in the eggs, tilting the pan slightly to coat the base evenly with the egg mixture.

3 Cook the eggs for a few seconds, until the base has set. Using a fork, stir gently – do not scramble – or push the sides slightly towards the middle to allow the uncooked egg mixture to run on to the hot pan and start cooking. Cook for about 1 minute, until just beginning to set.

4 Fold over one-third of the omelette with a large spatula. Tilting the pan away from you, flip the omelette over again and slide out on to a warm serving plate.

Cook's Tip

For the perfect omelette, the egg in the middle should still be slightly runny or creamy when served. If you prefer it more firmly set, cook it for a little longer in step 3.

Soufflé omelette

For this light and fluffy omelette the egg whites are whisked separately and then folded into the beaten yolk mixture before cooking. Serve the omelette immediately it is cooked, otherwise it will start to deflate.

1 In a large bowl, beat the egg yolks with seasoning or sugar, depending on whether you are making a savoury or sweet omelette. Whisk the egg white in a separate, grease-free bowl until stiff. Gently fold the egg whites into the yolk. Preheat the grill (broiler) to high.

2 Melt 15g/½oz/1 tbsp butter in an omelette pan or frying pan and spoon in the mixture, spreading it evenly.

3 Cook over a low heat for 2–3 minutes until golden on the underside and just firm on top. The omelette can be served as it is or held under the grill, slightly away from the heat as it will rise, and cooked for a few seconds until lightly browned on top.

4 Spoon the filling over one-third of the omelette, then use a large spatula to fold the omelette in half and transfer it to a warm serving plate.

THE FINISHING TOUCH

To add a professional-looking finish to a soufflé omelette, heat a greased skewer in a gas flame until almost glowing. (Make sure the skewer has a wooden handle and that you are wearing oven gloves.) Then press the skewer gently, but firmly, on the top of the omelette to mark diagonal lines. A sweet omelette can be dredged with icing (confectioners') sugar before being decorated.

OMELETTE FILLINGS

For a thin folded omelette, try sliced mushrooms or courgettes (zucchini), sautéed in a little butter; a sprinkling of grated cheese, such as Cheddar or Parmesan, with a little chopped parsley; or 30ml/2 tbsp chopped, smoked ham or cooked, shelled prawns (shrimp).

Sweet soufflé omelettes are best served with a fruit filling, such as a really good conserve, warmed with a splash or two of brandy or liqueur to help it spread, or try fresh raspberries, flamed in liqueur, with cream.

Cook's Tip

Combining whisked egg whites with yolks or other ingredients must be done very gently to avoid knocking out the air. A flexible rubber spatula is ideal, but a metal spoon works well too. Gently mix the ingredients in a figure-of-eight movement with a cutting, rather than stirring, action. When folding whisked egg whites into yolk mixtures, it is usual to stir a little of the white into the yolk to slacken the yolks before folding in the rest.

Making Thick-set Omelettes

Instead of folding or topping a lightly cooked thin omelette, the ingredients can be set in the beaten egg mixture. A much larger proportion of flavouring ingredients is used, often including vegetables, meat or fish and cheese. The mixture is cooked very slowly until firm, then either turned over and returned to the pan to cook the top side, or the omelette can be placed under a grill (broiler) to brown the top. The cooked omelette can be served hot, warm or cold, cut into wedges or slices. Spanish tortilla and Italian frittata are both types of set omelette.

Spanish tortilla

Easy, inexpensive and filling, this omelette is based on the widely available staples, onions and potatoes.

1 Heat 30ml/2 tbsp olive oil or a mixture of oil and butter in a large, heavy omelette or frying pan. Add about 450g/1lb thinly sliced potatoes and a large, thinly sliced onion and fry the potatoes and onions for 2–3 minutes, turning them frequently (the pan will be very full). Cover tightly and cook over a gentle heat for about 30 minutes, stirring occasionally, until the potatoes and onions are softened and slightly golden.

2 In a large mixing bowl, beat 6 eggs with salt and pepper, a crushed garlic clove and plenty of chopped fresh parsley. Gently stir in the potatoes and onions until well coated, taking care not to break up the potato slices too much. Wipe out the pan with kitchen paper and heat 30ml/2 tbsp more oil. Add the potato mixture and cook over a very low heat until the eggs have almost set.

3 Place a large heatproof plate, upside down, over the top of the pan. Holding them firmly together – use oven gloves or a thick cloth to protect your hands – carefully invert them.

4 Lift off the pan and allow the omelette to slip out on to the plate. Slide the omelette back into the pan, cooked side up, and continue cooking until set and golden underneath. Serve hot, warm or cold.

Italian frittata

This omelette is cooked with vegetables and cheese, and is served flat, like a Spanish tortilla. However, a frittata is usually thinner. Cut into wedges to serve.

1 Heat 30ml/2 tbsp oil in a large, heavy omelette or frying pan. Add a large sliced red onion and cook gently for 5 minutes, stirring occasionally until the onion is softened.

2 Add 350g/12oz diced, cooked new potatoes or courgettes (zucchini) and cook for 5 minutes until golden, stirring frequently, then spread the vegetables evenly over the base of the pan.

3 Preheat the grill (broiler) to high. Beat 6 eggs with salt and pepper, then pour the eggs over the hot vegetables. Sprinkle 115g/4oz cubed or grated cheese on top and cook over a moderate heat for about 5 minutes, or until the eggs are just set and the base of the frittata is lightly golden.

4 Place the pan under the preheated grill (protect the handle with a double layer of foil if it is not flameproof) and cook the top of the omelette for about 3 minutes until it is set and lightly golden. Serve hot, warm or cold.

THICK-SET OMELETTE FILLINGS
You can add a variety of extra ingredients to the basic recipes. Try a little lightly sautéed spinach, drained canned cannellini beans, steamed cauliflower florets, diced bacon or smoked ham or sliced spicy sausage. Alternatively, beat the eggs with 115g/4oz/1 cup grated Gruyère cheese before adding them to the pan.

Cook's Tip

If the egg mixture is very deep, then you can stir the egg and vegetable mixture very gently once or twice at the beginning of the cooking process to help set some of the egg, then spread out the mixture and cook until set.

Making Hot Soufflés

The top three tricks to a successful hot soufflé are to be sure that the oven has been preheated to the correct temperature before you put the dish into it, not to open the oven door during cooking and to have everyone seated at the table, ready for the soufflé as soon as it is cooked.

Basic hot soufflé

Most savoury hot soufflés are based on a thick white sauce. Before you begin, grease the inside of a soufflé dish and preheat the oven to 200°C/400°F/Gas 6.

1 Heat 300ml/½ pint/1¼ cups milk in a small pan to just below boiling point. Melt 25g/1oz/2 tbsp butter in a pan and stir in 25g/1oz/¼ cup plain (all-purpose) flour. Gradually whisk in the hot milk and bring to the boil, whisking constantly, until thickened. Remove the pan from the heat and leave to cool slightly so that the egg yolks don't cook when they are added. Beat in 4 egg yolks. Add the chosen flavourings, such as paprika, mustard and grated cheese, and stir until evenly mixed.

2 Whisk 4 egg whites in a grease-free bowl until stiff but not dry. Beat a spoonful of the whites into the egg yolk mixture to lighten it, then gently fold in the remaining whites.

3 Spoon the mixture into the prepared soufflé dish, taking care not to knock out the air. Run the tip of your finger around the top edge, just inside the rim, to make a narrow channel in the mixture. This will help the soufflé rise evenly.

4 If you like and depending on the type of soufflé, sprinkle a little freshly grated Parmesan cheese or fine breadcrumbs over the top. Place the dish in the oven in a position that allows sufficient room for the soufflé to rise and bake for 30–35 minutes. Serve immediately.

HOT SWEET SOUFFLÉS

These are made in a different way to savoury soufflés. A flavouring such as fruit purée or melted chocolate is folded into a stiff meringue mixture before baking.

Cook's Tips

• Do not delay putting the soufflé into the oven once it has been assembled, as this will prevent it from rising properly. However, you can do some of the preparation – up to the end of step 2 – in advance.

• To give a hot soufflé a cracked top or top hat effect, make a deep cut around the top of the mixture, about 1cm/½ in from the edge, with a spoon or knife before cooking.

Savoury soufflé roulade

A soufflé roulade is based on the basic soufflé mixture, which is then baked in a Swiss roll tin (jelly roll pan).

1 Grease and lightly dust the tin with flour or line it with non-stick baking parchment. Preheat the oven to 190°C/375°F/Gas 5.

2 Heat 300ml/½ pint/1¼ cups milk in a small pan to just below boiling point. Melt 25g/1oz/2 tbsp butter in a pan and stir in 25g/1oz/¼ cup plain (all-purpose) flour. Gradually whisk in the hot milk and bring to the boil, whisking constantly, until thickened. Remove the pan from the heat and leave to cool slightly. Beat in 4 egg yolks. Stir in the flavouring ingredients, such as grated cheese or spinach purée.

3 Whisk 4 egg whites in a grease-free bowl until stiff but not dry. Beat a spoonful of the whites into the egg yolk mixture to lighten it, then gently fold in the remaining egg whites. Pour the mixture into the tin and spread it evenly into the corners. Bake for 10–12 minutes until just firm to the touch.

4 Meanwhile, spread out a sheet of baking parchment on a clean dishtowel. Sprinkle it with freshly grated Parmesan cheese. Invert the roulade on to the paper and leave to cool slightly, then remove the lining paper.

5 Savoury roulades are best rolled up while hot, but they can also be rolled as they cool, using the dishtowel and paper as a support. Wrap the roulade in the dishtowel to keep it moist until you are ready to unroll it and add the filling.

SWEET SOUFFLÉ ROULADES

Like sweet soufflés, these are generally made using a meringue mixture. In a classic chocolate roulade, the egg yolks are beaten with half the sugar until light and fluffy, then melted chocolate and flavourings such as chestnut purée, liqueur or freshly brewed coffee are added. The egg whites are whisked until stiff with the remaining sugar and then folded into the chocolate mixture before baking. Sweet roulades are almost always rolled with the towel and paper inside, while warm, and then unrolled and filled with cream or custard when cold. An even simpler sweet roulade is based on soft-centred pavlova meringue.

Making Cold Soufflés

Iced and cold soufflés are a grander version of a mousse. They are fluffier, lightened with whisked egg white and set with gelatine, then piled into a soufflé dish surrounded by a collar of paper to support the mixture and give a "risen" appearance. Cold soufflés can be served chilled or part-frozen. They are easier to make than their appearance suggests and they are sure to impress your guests.

Cold sweet soufflé

1 Attach a collar to the soufflé dish and coat the inside of the dish, if you like. Whisk 75g/3oz/generous ⅓ cup caster (superfine) sugar with 6 large (US extra large) egg yolks until thick and pale. Heat 250ml/8fl oz/1 cup milk to just below boiling point, then whisk it into the egg yolk mixture. Return to the pan and stir over a low heat until the mixture is thick enough to coat the back of the spoon. Remove the pan from the heat.

2 Sprinkle 15ml/1 tbsp powdered gelatine over 45ml/3 tbsp water in a heatproof bowl and set aside for 5 minutes. Add the soaked gelatine to the hot custard and stir until melted. Stir in the flavouring, such as coffee essence, mocha syrup or sieved crushed fruit. Mix thoroughly, then chill.

3 When the mixture is beginning to set, lightly whisk the egg whites until foamy. Gradually whisk in 115g/4oz/generous ½ cup caster sugar until stiff and glossy. Fold the egg whites into the custard with a spatula or balloon whisk.

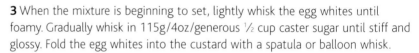

4 When the mixture is nearly set and just beginning to hold its shape when stirred, pour it into the prepared dish. It should reach about 5cm/2in above the rim. Chill until set. If you are making an iced soufflé, freeze for at least 1 hour. When ready to serve, carefully and slowly peel off the collar.

COLD SAVOURY SOUFFLÉS

These can be made by the same basic method as a cold sweet soufflé, using a plain savoury sauce or purée of ingredients as the base. Dissolve the gelatine into the flavouring mixture, stir into the savoury sauce, then allow to part-set before folding in the whisked egg whites.

MAKING A SOUFFLÉ COLLAR

Although some cooks prefer to do so, it is not necessary to tie a collar around the dish for a hot soufflé, as the mixture will support itself. However, a collar is essential when making a cold soufflé as the mixture is poured in to a level above the rim of the dish.

For a neat finish and to avoid having any mixture leaking down between the paper and the dish, the collar must be attached firmly. Cut a strip of baking parchment or greaseproof (waxed) paper long enough to wrap around the dish with a small overlap and wide enough to stand about 7.5cm/3in above the rim, when it has been folded in half lengthways. Fold the paper in half to provide a double thickness. Attach one end to the dish with tape, wrap the collar tightly and evenly around the dish and secure the other end with tape. Tie the paper in place with string.

COATING THE SOUFFLÉ DISH

To give cold soufflés additional flavour, coat the inside of the dish before adding the mixture. Finely grated chocolate would complement a sweet coffee soufflé, while freshly grated Parmesan cheese or fine toasted breadcrumbs go well with a savoury soufflé. Butter the dish well, then shake the coating all over the inside. Tip out any excess.

DECORATING A SOUFFLÉ

The sides of a cold soufflé can be coated to decorate. Grated chocolate, crushed praline, flaked (sliced) almonds or chopped pistachio nuts are all suitable for sweet soufflés, while grated cheese, toasted breadcrumbs or chopped nuts would suit savoury soufflés. Press the coating on the soufflé using a cake slice.

Cook's Tip

If the collar on a cold soufflé does not come away easily, use a warm, round-bladed knife to loosen it. Hold the warm knife on the paper collar for a few seconds to melt the edge of the soufflé slightly, then ease the paper away. Continue all the way round the soufflé.

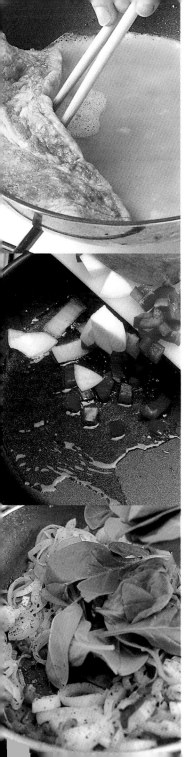

Savoury Omelettes & Frittatas

Spanning the globe from East to West, these mouthwatering recipes really show off the versatility of the ever-popular omelette. Some are ideal for an easy midweek supper, others make terrific snacks to serve with drinks, while still more make picnics perfect.

Chinese Omelette Parcels with Stir-fried Vegetables

Stir-fried vegetables in black bean sauce make a really unusual and remarkably good omelette filling.

INGREDIENTS

130g/4½oz broccoli, cut into
  small florets
30ml/2 tbsp groundnut
  (peanut) oil
1cm/½in piece of fresh root
  ginger, finely grated
1 large garlic clove, crushed
2 red chillies, seeded and
  thinly sliced
4 spring onions (scallions),
  sliced diagonally
175g/6oz/3 cups pak choi
  (bok choy), shredded
50g/2oz/2 cups fresh
  coriander (cilantro) leaves,
  plus extra to garnish
115g/4oz/2 cups beansprouts
45ml/3 tbsp black bean sauce
4 eggs
salt and ground black pepper

Cook's Tip
*Black bean sauce is available
in jars or cans from Chinese and
Asian food stores and most
large supermarkets.*

1 Blanch the broccoli in salted, boiling water for 2 minutes, drain well, then refresh under cold running water.

2 Meanwhile, heat 15ml/1 tbsp of the oil in a frying pan or wok. Add the ginger, garlic and half the chilli and stir-fry for 1 minute. Add the spring onions, broccoli and pak choi and stir-fry for 2 minutes more, tossing the vegetables constantly to prevent them sticking and to cook them evenly.

3 Chop three-quarters of the coriander and add to the frying pan or wok. Add the beansprouts and stir-fry for 1 minute, then add the black bean sauce and heat through for 1 minute more. Remove the pan from the heat and keep warm.

4 Mix the eggs lightly with a fork and season well. Heat a little of the remaining oil in a small frying pan and add one-quarter of the beaten egg. Swirl the egg until it covers the base of the pan, then sprinkle over one-quarter of the reserved coriander leaves. Cook until set, then turn out on to a plate and keep warm while you make three more omelettes, adding more oil, when necessary.

5 Spoon the vegetable stir-fry on to the omelettes and roll up. Cut in half crossways and serve garnished with coriander leaves and chilli.

Japanese Rolled Omelette

Much easier than it looks – all that is needed to make this fabulously light omelette is a sushi rolling mat.

1 Combine the dashi, mirin, sugar, shoyu and salt. Add the mixture to the beaten eggs and stir well.

2 Heat a round omelette pan or a rectangular Japanese pan over a medium heat. Soak kitchen paper in a little oil and wipe the pan to grease it. Pour in one-quarter of the egg mixture. Tilt the pan to coat it evenly. When the omelette starts to set, roll it up towards you with chopsticks or a spatula.

3 Push the rolled omelette to the farthest side of the pan from you. Oil the empty part of the pan again. Pour one-third of the egg mixture in at the empty side. Lift up the first roll with chopsticks, and let the egg mixture run underneath. When it looks half set, roll the omelette around the first roll.

4 Move the roll gently on to a sushi rolling mat covered with clear film (plastic wrap). Roll the omelette firmly into the roller mat. Leave to stand rolled up for 5 minutes. Repeat the whole process again to make another roll. Then cut the rolled omelettes crossways into 2.5cm/1in slices.

5 Finely grate the mooli. Squeeze out the juice with your hand. Lay the shiso leaves, if using, on four plates and place a few slices of the omelette on top. Put a small heap of grated mooli to one side and add a few drops of shoyu.

SERVES FOUR

INGREDIENTS
45ml/3 tbsp dashi stock
   or the same amount of
   water and a pinch
   of dashi-no-moto
30ml/2 tbsp mirin
15ml/1 tbsp caster
   (superfine) sugar
5ml/1 tsp shoyu
5ml/1 tsp salt
6 large (US extra large)
   eggs, beaten
vegetable oil

To garnish
2.5cm/1in mooli (daikon)
4 shiso leaves (optional)
shoyu

Thick-set Omelette with Spicy Sausage

This colourful, Spanish-style omelette is great hot or cold. Cut into wedges and serve with a fresh tomato and basil salad.

SERVES FOUR TO SIX

INGREDIENTS

75ml/5 tbsp olive oil

175g/6oz chorizo or spicy sausage, thinly sliced

675g/1½lb potatoes, peeled and thinly sliced

275g/10oz onions, halved and thinly sliced

4 eggs

30ml/2 tbsp chopped fresh parsley, plus extra to garnish

115g/4oz/1 cup grated Cheddar cheese

salt and ground black pepper

1 Heat 15ml/1 tbsp of the oil in a non-stick frying pan, about 20cm/8in in diameter, and cook the sausage until golden brown and cooked through. Lift out with a slotted spoon and drain thoroughly on kitchen paper.

2 Add a further 30ml/2 tbsp oil to the pan and cook the potatoes and onions for 2–3 minutes, turning frequently (the pan will be very full). Cover tightly and cook over a gentle heat for about 30 minutes, turning occasionally, until softened and slightly golden.

3 Mix the eggs with the parsley, cheese, sausage and plenty of seasoning in a large bowl. Gently stir in the potatoes and onions until well coated in the egg and cheese mixture, taking care not to break up the potato slices too much.

4 Wipe out the pan with kitchen paper and heat the remaining 30ml/2 tbsp oil. Add the egg and potato mixture and cook over a very low heat until the egg begins to set. Use a spatula to prevent the omelette from sticking to the sides.

5 Preheat the grill (broiler) to hot. When the base of the omelette has set, which should take about 5 minutes, protect the pan handle with foil and place under the grill until the top is set and golden. Cut into wedges and serve garnished with parsley.

Spanish Omelette with White Beans

This authentic variation from northern Spain makes a terrific supper for hungry vegetarians.

1 Heat the olive oil in a 30cm/12in frying pan or paella pan. Add the onion, red pepper and celery, and cook for 3–5 minutes until the vegetables are soft, but not coloured.

2 Add the potatoes and beans and cook for several minutes to heat through.

3 In a small bowl, beat the eggs with a fork, then season well with salt and pepper and pour the egg mixture over the ingredients in the pan.

4 Stir the egg mixture with a wooden spatula until it begins to thicken, then cook over a low heat for about 8 minutes. The omelette should be firm, but still moist in the middle. Cool slightly then invert on to a serving plate.

5 Cut the omelette into thick wedges. Serve warm or cool garnished with fresh oregano sprigs and accompanied by a green salad with olives and a little olive oil to drizzle over.

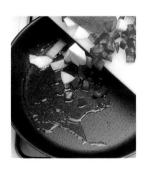

SERVES SIX

INGREDIENTS

30ml/2 tbsp olive oil, plus
   extra for drizzling
1 Spanish (Bermuda)
   onion, chopped
1 small red (bell) pepper,
   seeded and diced
2 celery sticks, chopped
225g/8oz potatoes, peeled,
   diced and cooked
400g/14oz can cannellini
   beans, drained
8 eggs
salt and ground black pepper
oregano, to garnish
green salad and olives,
   to serve

Cook's Tip

In Spain, this omelette is often served as tapas and would also make a good appetizer. It is delicious served cold, cut into bitesize pieces and accompanied by a spicy chilli sauce or creamy mayonnaise for dipping.

Potato and Onion Tortilla with Broad Beans

This is a very summery dish to enjoy at lunch. Alternatively, cut it into small pieces and serve as a Spanish tapas when you are entertaining informally and want to do something different.

SERVES TWO

INGREDIENTS

45ml/3 tbsp olive oil
2 Spanish (Bermuda) onions, thinly sliced
300g/11oz waxy potatoes, cut into 1cm/½in dice
250g/9oz/1¾ cups shelled broad (fava) beans
5ml/1 tsp chopped fresh thyme or summer savory
6 large (US extra large) eggs
45ml/3 tbsp mixed chopped chives and chopped flat leaf parsley
salt and ground black pepper

1 Heat 30ml/2 tbsp of the oil in a deep 23cm/9in non-stick frying pan. Add the onions and potatoes and stir to coat. Cover and cook gently, stirring frequently, for 20–25 minutes until the potatoes are cooked and the onions collapsed. Do not let the mixture brown.

2 Meanwhile, cook the beans in a pan of salted, boiling water for 5 minutes. Drain well and set aside until the beans are cool enough to handle, then peel off the grey-green outer skins and discard.

3 Add the beans to the frying pan, together with the thyme or summer savory and season with salt and pepper to taste. Stir well to mix and cook for a further 2–3 minutes until heated through.

4 Beat the eggs in a bowl with salt and pepper to taste. Stir in the mixed herbs, then pour the egg mixture over the potatoes and onions and increase the heat slightly. Cook gently until the underside sets and browns, gently pulling the omelette away from the sides of the pan and tilting it to allow the uncooked egg to run underneath.

5 Invert the tortilla on to a plate. Add the remaining oil to the pan and heat until hot. Slip the tortilla back into the pan, uncooked side down, and cook for another 3–4 minutes to allow the underneath to brown. Slide the tortilla out on to a plate. Divide as you like and serve warm rather than piping hot.

Frittata with Leek, Red Pepper and Spinach

This glorious combination of eggs, sweet leeks, red pepper and spinach seems to melt in the mouth in a quite magical way.

SERVES THREE
TO FOUR

INGREDIENTS

30ml/2 tbsp olive oil
1 large red (bell) pepper, seeded and diced
2.5–5ml/½–1 tsp ground cumin
3 leeks (about 450g/1lb in total), thinly sliced
150g/5oz baby spinach leaves
45ml/3 tbsp pine nuts, toasted
5 large (US extra large) eggs
15ml/1 tbsp chopped fresh basil
15ml/1 tbsp chopped fresh flat leaf parsley
salt and ground black pepper
watercress, to garnish
50g/2oz/⅔ cup freshly grated Parmesan cheese, to serve (optional)

1 Heat a heavy, non-stick frying pan and add the olive oil. Add the red pepper and cook over a medium heat, stirring occasionally, for 6–8 minutes, until soft. Stir in 2.5ml/½ tsp of the ground cumin and cook for a further 1–2 minutes.

2 Stir in the leeks, then partly cover the pan and cook gently for 5 minutes, or until the leeks have softened and collapsed. Season with salt and pepper.

3 Add the spinach and cover the pan. Allow the spinach to wilt in the steam for 3–4 minutes, then stir to mix it into the vegetables, adding the pine nuts.

4 Beat the eggs with salt, pepper, the remaining cumin, basil and parsley. Add to the pan and cook over a gentle heat until the base of the omelette sets and turns golden brown. Pull the edges of the omelette away from the sides of the pan as it cooks and tilt the pan so that the uncooked egg runs underneath.

5 Preheat the grill (broiler). Flash the frittata under the hot grill to set the egg on top, but do not let it become too brown. Cut the frittata into wedges and serve warm, garnished with watercress and sprinkled with Parmesan, if using.

Variation

A delicious way to serve frittata is to pack it into a slightly hollowed-out loaf and then drizzle it with extra virgin olive oil. Wrap tightly in clear film (plastic wrap) and leave to stand for 1–2 hours before cutting into slices.

Frittata with Sun-dried Tomatoes

To savour the colours and flavours of the Mediterranean serve this tasty Italian dish warm for an *al fresco* lunch or pack it in a picnic basket to eat cold in the countryside or at the coast.

1 Place the tomatoes in a small bowl and pour in enough hot water just to cover them. Leave to soak for about 15 minutes. Lift the tomatoes out of the water with a slotted spoon and pat dry on kitchen paper. Reserve the tomato soaking water. Cut the tomatoes into thin strips.

2 Heat the oil in a large, non-stick frying pan. Stir in the chopped onion and cook for 5–6 minutes, or until softened and golden. Stir in the sun-dried tomatoes and thyme and cook over a medium heat for a further 2–3 minutes, stirring occasionally. Season with salt and ground black pepper.

3 Break the eggs into a bowl and beat lightly. Stir in 45ml/3 tbsp of the tomato soaking water and the Parmesan. Increase the heat under the pan. When the oil is sizzling, add the eggs. Mix quickly into the other ingredients, then stop stirring. Lower the heat to medium and cook for 4–5 minutes, or until the base is golden and the top puffed.

4 Place a large plate upside down over the pan and, holding it firmly, turn the pan and the frittata over on to it. Slide the frittata back into the pan and continue cooking for 3–4 minutes, until golden brown on the second side. Remove the pan from the heat. Cut the frittata into wedges, garnish and serve.

SERVES THREE
TO FOUR

INGREDIENTS
6 sun-dried tomatoes
60ml/4 tbsp olive oil
1 small onion, finely chopped
pinch of fresh thyme leaves
6 eggs
50g/2oz/^{2}/$_3$ cup freshly
   grated Parmesan cheese
salt and ground black pepper
fresh thyme sprigs, to garnish
shavings of Parmesan,
   to serve

Savoury Soufflés

Fabulous, fluffy and fun, savoury soufflés never fail to impress, whether classics flavoured with cheese or mushrooms or something a little more exotic with spicy seafood. The dishes featured here also include a melt-in-the-mouth roulade.

Classic Cheese Soufflé

A light, delicate, melt-in-the-mouth cheese soufflé makes one of the most delightful brunches imaginable. All you need to go with it is salad, a glass – or two – of good wine and plenty of time to relax and enjoy a lazy weekend.

**SERVES TWO
TO THREE**

INGREDIENTS

50g/2oz/¼ cup butter
30–45ml/2–3 tbsp dried,
    fine breadcrumbs
200ml/7fl oz/scant
    1 cup milk
30g/1¼oz/3 tbsp plain
    (all-purpose) flour
pinch of cayenne pepper
2.5ml/½ tsp mustard powder
50g/2oz/½ cup grated
    mature (sharp)
    Cheddar cheese
25g/1oz/⅓ cup freshly
    grated Parmesan cheese
4 eggs, separated, plus
    1 egg white
salt and ground black pepper

Variation

You can use just about any hard cheese instead of Cheddar – whatever is your favourite. Try Red Leicester, Gruyère, Mahon, Provolone, Gouda or Kefalotiri.

1 Preheat the oven to 190°C/375°F/Gas 5. Melt 15ml/1 tbsp of the butter and grease a 1.2 litre/ 2 pint/5 cup soufflé dish. Coat with breadcrumbs.

2 Heat the milk in a large pan. Add the remaining butter, the flour, cayenne and mustard powder. Bring to the boil over a low heat, whisking steadily until the mixture thickens to a smooth sauce.

3 Simmer the sauce for 1–2 minutes, then turn off the heat and whisk in all the Cheddar and half the Parmesan. Cool a little, then beat in the egg yolks. Check the seasoning. Set aside.

4 Whisk the egg whites in a large grease-free bowl until they form soft, glossy peaks. Add a few spoonfuls of the beaten egg whites to the sauce to lighten it. Beat well, then tip the rest of the whites into the pan and, with a large metal spoon, gently fold them in.

5 Pour the mixture into the prepared soufflé dish, level the top and, to help the soufflé rise evenly, run your fingertip around the inside rim of the dish.

6 Place the dish on a baking sheet. Sprinkle the remaining Parmesan over the top of the soufflé mixture and bake for about 25 minutes until risen and golden brown. Serve immediately.

Goat's Cheese Soufflé

Goat's cheese ranges in flavour from the mild and creamy to the strong and tangy. Whichever you choose, this sophisticated soufflé is delicious served with a crisp, white wine.

1 Melt the butter in a heavy pan over a medium heat. Stir in the flour and cook until slightly golden, stirring occasionally. Pour in half the milk, stir until smooth, then add the remaining milk and the bay leaf. Season with salt, pepper and nutmeg. Reduce the heat to medium-low, then cover and simmer gently for about 5 minutes, stirring occasionally.

2 Preheat the oven to 190°C/375°F/Gas 5. Butter a 1.5 litre/2½ pint/6¼ cup soufflé dish and sprinkle with Parmesan cheese. Remove the sauce from the heat and discard the bay leaf. Stir in the other cheeses.

3 In a clean grease-free bowl, gently beat the egg whites until frothy. Add the cream of tartar, increase the speed and continue beating until they form stiff peaks that just flop over a little at the top.

4 Stir a spoonful of beaten egg whites into the cheese sauce to lighten it, then pour the cheese sauce over the rest of the whites.

5 Gently fold the sauce into the whites. Pour the soufflé mixture into the prepared dish and bake for about 30 minutes until puffed and golden brown. Serve immediately.

SERVES FOUR

INGREDIENTS

25g/1oz/2 tbsp butter, plus
   extra for greasing
25g/1oz/¼ cup plain
   (all-purpose) flour
175ml/6fl oz/¾ cup milk
1 bay leaf
freshly grated nutmeg
freshly grated Parmesan
   cheese, for sprinkling
40g/1½oz herb and garlic
   soft cheese
150g/5oz/1¼ cups diced
   firm goat's cheese
6 egg whites, at
   room temperature
1.5ml/¼ tsp cream of tartar
salt and ground black pepper

Variation
Use a blue cheese, such as Roquefort or Stilton, instead of goat's cheese.

Cheese and Tomato Soufflés

Guests are always phenomenally impressed with a home-made soufflé and this recipe for little individual ones is the ultimate in effortless entertaining. You don't have to tell them that you used a ready-made sauce.

SERVES SIX

INGREDIENTS

350g/12oz tub fresh
   cheese sauce
50g/2oz sun-dried tomatoes
   in olive oil, drained, plus
   10ml/2 tsp of the oil
130g/4½oz/1½ cups grated
   Parmesan cheese
4 large (US extra large)
   eggs, separated
salt and ground black pepper

Variations

Cheese goes well with a variety of flavours, so instead of using sun-dried tomatoes, try a mixture of sliced black olives and drained capers, chopped anchovies, chopped walnuts or fresh herbs, such as parsley, tarragon, fennel or dill.

1 Preheat the oven to 200°C/400°F/Gas 6. Tip the cheese sauce into a bowl. Thinly slice the sun-dried tomatoes and add them to the sauce with 90g/3½oz/ generous 1 cup of the Parmesan and the egg yolks. Season well with salt and pepper and stir until thoroughly combined.

2 Brush the base and sides of six 200ml/7fl oz/scant 1 cup ramekins or individual soufflé dishes with the oil, then divide about half of the remaining Parmesan cheese among the dishes. Coat the insides of the dishes with the cheese, tilting them until evenly covered. Tip out any excess cheese and set aside with the reserved cheese.

3 Whisk the egg whites in a clean, grease-free bowl until stiff. Use a large metal spoon to stir one-quarter of the egg whites into the sauce, stirring gently until evenly blended, then fold in the remaining egg whites.

4 Spoon the mixture into the prepared ramekins or dishes and sprinkle with the reserved cheese. Place the soufflé dishes on a baking sheet and bake for 15–18 minutes until well risen and golden. Serve immediately.

Wild Mushroom and Sun-dried Tomato Soufflés

These impressive little soufflés are packed with rich, Italian flavours and smell unbelievably appetizing as they are cooking.

1 Place the ceps in a bowl, pour over warm water to cover and leave to soak for about 15 minutes. Grease four individual earthenware soufflé dishes with a little butter. Sprinkle the grated Parmesan into the soufflé dishes and rotate each dish to coat the sides with cheese, then tip out any excess cheese and set the dishes aside. Preheat the oven to 190°C/375°F/Gas 5.

2 Melt the butter in a large pan, remove from the heat and stir in the flour. Return to a low heat and cook for 1 minute, stirring constantly. Remove the pan from the heat and gradually stir in the milk. Return to the heat and bring to the boil, stirring constantly, until the sauce has thickened.

3 Remove the sauce from the heat, then stir in the Cheddar and seasoning. Beat in the egg yolks, one at a time, then stir in the sun-dried tomatoes and chives. Drain the soaked mushrooms, coarsely chop them and add to the sauce.

4 Whisk the egg whites until they stand in soft peaks. Mix one spoonful into the sauce, then carefully fold in the remainder. Divide the mixture among the soufflé dishes and bake for 25 minutes, or until the soufflés are golden brown on top, well risen and just firm to the touch. Serve immediately.

SERVES FOUR

INGREDIENTS

25g/1oz/½ cup dried
   cep mushrooms
40g/1½oz/3 tbsp butter, plus
   extra for greasing
20ml/4 tsp freshly grated
   Parmesan cheese
40g/1½oz/⅓ cup plain
   (all-purpose) flour
250ml/8fl oz/1 cup milk
50g/2oz/½ cup grated
   mature (sharp)
   Cheddar cheese
4 eggs, separated
2 sun-dried tomatoes in oil,
   drained and chopped
15ml/1 tbsp chopped
   fresh chives
salt and ground black pepper

Cook's Tip

Ceps are also known by their Italian name, porcini. A variety of different dried mushrooms are available – any can be used instead of the ceps.

Hot Crab Soufflés

Spiced with Thai flavourings, these luxurious little soufflés would make an unusual and elegant appetizer for a dinner party, but are just as good served with salad for lunch.

SERVES SIX

INGREDIENTS

50g/2oz/¼ cup butter

45ml/3 tbsp fine
   wholemeal (whole-
   wheat) breadcrumbs

4 spring onions (scallions),
   finely chopped

15ml/1 tbsp Malaysian or
   mild Madras curry powder

25g/1oz/¼ cup plain
   (all-purpose) flour

105ml/7 tbsp coconut milk
   or milk

150ml/¼ pint/⅔ cup
   whipping cream

4 egg yolks

225g/8oz white crab meat

mild green Tabasco sauce

6 egg whites

salt and ground black pepper

Variation

*Cooked lobster meat or salmon
fillet can be used instead of
crab in these soufflés.*

1 Use some of the butter to grease six ramekins or a 1.75 litre/3 pint/7½ cup soufflé dish. Sprinkle in the breadcrumbs, roll the dishes or dish around to coat the base and sides completely, then tip out the excess breadcrumbs. Preheat the oven to 200°C/400°F/Gas 6.

2 Melt the remaining butter in a pan, add the spring onions and Malaysian or mild Madras curry powder and cook over a low heat for about 1 minute until the spring onions have softened. Stir in the flour and cook for 1 minute more.

3 Gradually add the coconut milk or milk and cream, stirring constantly. Cook until smooth and thick. Remove the pan from the heat, stir in the egg yolks, then the crab. Season with salt, black pepper and Tabasco sauce.

4 In a grease-free bowl, beat the egg whites with a pinch of salt until stiff. Using a metal spoon, stir one-third into the mixture to lighten it, then fold in the rest. Spoon into the dishes or dish.

5 Bake until well risen and golden brown and just firm to the touch. The individual soufflés will be ready in about 8 minutes; a large soufflé will take 15–20 minutes. Serve immediately.

Twice-baked Cheese Soufflés

These cute, little soufflés can be prepared up to a day in advance, then reheated in the sauce just before serving – ideal for easy, stress-free entertaining.

1 Preheat the oven to 190°C/375°F/Gas 5. Lightly grease six 175ml/6fl oz/ ¾ cup ramekins, then line the bases with buttered greaseproof (waxed) paper.

2 Melt the butter in a small pan, stir in the flour and cook for 1 minute, stirring. Gradually whisk in the milk. Add the bay leaf and season. Bring to the boil and cook, stirring, for 1 minute. Remove the pan from the heat and discard the bay leaf. Beat in the egg yolks, one at a time, then stir in the cheese.

3 Gently whisk the egg whites until frothy. Add the cream of tartar, then whisk vigorously until they form soft peaks. Whisk a spoonful of the whites into the cheese sauce, then pour the sauce over the remaining whites and gently fold in.

4 Spoon the mixture into the ramekins. Put them in an ovenproof dish and pour in boiling water to halfway up the sides. Bake for 18 minutes, until puffed and golden. Let the soufflés cool just long enough for them to deflate.

5 Increase the oven temperature to 220°C/425°F/Gas 7. Run a knife around the edge of the soufflés and invert on to an ovenproof dish. Remove the lining paper. Season the cream and pour over the soufflés, sprinkle with almonds and bake for 10–15 minutes until well risen and golden. Garnish and serve.

SERVES SIX

INGREDIENTS

20g/¾oz/1½ tbsp butter, plus extra for greasing
30ml/2 tbsp plain (all-purpose) flour
150ml/¼ pint/⅔ cup milk
1 small bay leaf
2 eggs, separated, plus 1 egg white, at room temperature
115g/4oz/1 cup grated Gruyère cheese
1.5ml/¼ tsp cream of tartar
250ml/8fl oz/1 cup double (heavy) cream
25g/1oz/¼ cup flaked (sliced) almonds
salt, ground black pepper and grated nutmeg
fresh parsley sprigs, to garnish
salad leaves, to serve

Spinach and Goat's Cheese Roulade

Roulades are now back in fashion – and one bite of this crisp coated, light-as-air savoury roll will demonstrate why.

SERVES FOUR

INGREDIENTS

150g/5oz/10 tbsp butter,
   plus extra for greasing
300ml/½ pint/1¼ cups milk
50g/2oz/½ cup plain
   (all-purpose) flour
100g/3¾oz chèvre (goat's
   cheese), chopped
40g/1½oz/½ cup freshly
   grated Parmesan cheese,
   plus extra for dusting
4 eggs, separated
250g/9oz/3⅔ cups shiitake
   mushrooms, sliced
275g/10oz baby spinach
   leaves, washed
45ml/3 tbsp crème fraîche
salt and ground black pepper

Cook's Tip

*Use thick double (heavy) cream
or sour cream in place of the
crème fraîche, if you like.*

1 Preheat the oven to 190°C/375°F/Gas 5. Line a 30 × 20cm/12 × 8in Swiss roll tin (jelly roll pan) with greaseproof (waxed) paper, making sure that the edge of the paper rises well above the sides of the tin. Grease lightly.

2 Combine the milk, flour and 50g/2oz/¼ cup of the butter in a pan. Gradually bring to the boil, whisking until smooth. Simmer for 2 minutes, then stir in the chèvre and half the Parmesan. Cool for 5 minutes. Beat in the egg yolks. Season.

3 Whisk the egg whites until soft peaks form, then fold into the chèvre mixture. Spoon the mixture into the tin, spread to level, then bake for 15 minutes until the top feels just firm.

4 Dust a sheet of greaseproof paper with Parmesan and carefully invert the roulade on to the paper. Tear off the lining paper in strips. Roll up the roulade in the greaseproof paper and set aside to cool.

5 To make the filling, melt the rest of the butter in a pan, reserving 30ml/2 tbsp. Stir-fry the mushrooms for 3 minutes. In a separate pan, cook the spinach until it wilts. Drain well, add to the mushrooms and stir in the crème fraîche. Season, then cool. Preheat the oven to the original temperature.

6 Unroll the roulade and spread over the filling. Roll it up again and place on a baking sheet. Brush with the reserved butter and sprinkle with the remaining Parmesan. Bake for 15 minutes until risen and golden. Serve immediately.

Dessert Soufflés & Omelettes

Flamboyantly fruity or wildly wicked, these fabulous hot and cold desserts are just dreamy. As easy to make as their savoury cousins, they are ideal for entertaining as they look and taste so stunningly special.

Frozen Grand Marnier Soufflés

Light and fluffy, yet almost ice cream, these wickedly indulgent soufflés are perfect for a special dinner party. As you need to allow time for freezing, all the hard work is done in advance. Redcurrants or other soft fruits make a delicious decoration.

SERVES EIGHT

INGREDIENTS

200g/7oz/1 cup caster
  (superfine) sugar
6 large (US extra large)
  eggs, separated
250ml/8fl oz/1 cup milk
15g/¹⁄₂oz/1 tbsp powdered
  gelatine, soaked in 45ml/
  3 tbsp cold water
450ml/³⁄₄ pint/scant 2 cups
  double (heavy) cream
60ml/4 tbsp Grand Marnier

Cook's Tip

The soft ball stage of a syrup is when a teaspoon of the mixture dropped into a glass of cold water sets into a soft ball.

Variation

If you prefer, you can make just one dessert in a large soufflé dish, rather than eight individual desserts.

1 Wrap a double collar of greaseproof (waxed) paper around eight dessert glasses or ramekins and tie with string. Whisk 75g/3oz/generous ¹⁄₃ cup of the caster sugar with the egg yolks until the yolks are pale. This will take about 5 minutes by hand or about 3 minutes with an electric hand mixer.

2 Heat the milk until almost boiling and pour it on to the yolks, whisking constantly. Return to the pan and stir over a low heat until thick enough to coat the back of the spoon. Remove the pan from the heat. Stir the soaked gelatine into the custard. Pour the custard into a bowl and leave to cool. Whisk occasionally until on the point of setting.

3 Put the remaining sugar in a pan with 45ml/ 3 tbsp water and dissolve it over a low heat. Bring to the boil and boil rapidly until it reaches the soft ball stage or 119°C/238°F on a sugar thermometer. Remove the pan from the heat. In a clean bowl, whisk the egg whites until stiff. Pour the hot syrup on to the whites, whisking constantly. Leave to cool.

4 Add the Grand Marnier to the cold custard. Whisk the cream until it holds soft peaks and fold into the cooled meringue, with the custard. Pour the mixture into the prepared glasses or dishes. Freeze overnight. Remove the paper collars and leave at room temperature for 15 minutes before serving.

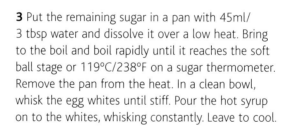

Cold Lemon Soufflé with Almonds

Easy on the eye and easy to make, this refreshing dessert soufflé is light and mouthwatering – ideal for the end of any meal.

1 Wrap a baking parchment collar around a 900ml/ 1½ pint/3¾ cup soufflé dish so that it extends 7.5cm/3in above the rim. Tape, then tie with string. Lightly coat the inside of the collar with oil.

2 Whisk together the lemon rind, egg yolks and 75g/3oz/6 tbsp of the sugar until light and creamy.

3 Place the lemon juice in a heatproof bowl and sprinkle over the gelatine. Set aside for 5 minutes, then set over a pan of simmering water, stirring occasionally, until dissolved. Cool slightly, then stir into the egg yolk mixture. Fold in the cream.

4 Whisk the whites to stiff peaks. Gradually whisk in the remaining sugar until stiff and glossy. Fold the whites into the yolk mixture. Pour into the prepared dish, smooth the surface and chill for 4–5 hours.

5 To make the almond topping, lightly oil a baking sheet. Preheat the grill (broiler). Spread the almonds over the baking sheet and sift over the icing sugar. Grill (broil) until they are golden and caramelized. Cool, then remove the almond mixture from the tray with a metal spatula and break it into pieces.

6 When the soufflé has set, carefully peel off the collar. Sprinkle the caramelized almonds on top of the soufflé to serve.

SERVES SIX

INGREDIENTS
oil, for greasing
grated rind and juice of
    3 large lemons
5 large (US extra large)
    eggs, separated
115g/4oz/generous ½ cup
    caster (superfine) sugar
25ml/1½ tbsp
    powdered gelatine
450ml/¾ pint/scant 2 cups
    double (heavy) cream,
    lightly whipped

For the almond topping
75g/3oz/¾ cup flaked
    (sliced) almonds
75g/3oz/¾ cup icing
    (confectioners') sugar

Cook's Tip
To dissolve the gelatine more quickly, heat the lemon juice and gelatine in a microwave, on full power, in 30-second bursts, stirring between each burst, until it is fully dissolved.

Chilled Coffee and Praline Soufflé

A smooth coffee soufflé with a crushed praline topping that is spectacular and sophisticated.

INGREDIENTS

oil, for greasing

150g/5oz/³⁄₄ cup caster
(superfine) sugar

75ml/5 tbsp water

150g/5oz/generous 1 cup
blanched almonds, plus
extra for decoration

120ml/4fl oz/¹⁄₂ cup strong
brewed coffee, such as
hazelnut-flavoured

15ml/1 tbsp powdered
gelatine

3 eggs, separated

75g/3oz/scant ¹⁄₂ cup soft
light brown sugar

15ml/1 tbsp coffee liqueur,
such as Tia Maria, Kahlúa
or Toussaint

150ml/¹⁄₄ pint/²⁄₃ cup double
(heavy) cream, plus extra,
whipped, for decoration
(optional)

1 Wrap a greaseproof (waxed) paper collar around a 900ml/1¹⁄₂ pint/3³⁄₄ cup soufflé dish that extends 5cm/2in above the rim, tape to secure, then tie in place with string. Chill the dish.

2 Oil a baking sheet. Put the caster sugar and water in a small heavy pan and heat gently until the sugar dissolves. Boil rapidly until the syrup becomes pale golden. Add the almonds and boil until dark golden. Pour the mixture on to the baking sheet and leave to set. When hard, transfer to a plastic bag and break into pieces with a rolling pin. Reserve 50g/2oz/¹⁄₂ cup and crush the remainder.

3 Pour half the coffee into a heatproof bowl. Sprinkle over the gelatine. Leave for 5 minutes, then set over a pan of simmering water, stirring until dissolved.

4 Whisk the egg yolks, brown sugar, remaining coffee and liqueur in a heatproof bowl over a pan of simmering water until thick. Whisk in the gelatine. Whip the cream to soft peaks. Stiffly whisk the egg whites. Fold the crushed praline into the cream, then fold into the coffee mixture. Fold in the whites, half at a time.

5 Spoon into the soufflé dish and smooth the top. Chill for 2 hours, or until set. Put in the freezer for 15–20 minutes before serving. Remove the paper collar. Decorate with whipped cream, if using, praline pieces and almonds.

Fruit-filled Soufflé Omelette

This attractive and scrumptious dessert is surprisingly quick and easy to make. The creamy omelette fluffs up in the pan, flops over to envelop its filling of fruits in liqueur and then slides gracefully on to the plate.

1 Hull the strawberries, cut them in half and place them in a bowl. Pour over 30ml/2 tbsp of the liqueur and set aside to macerate.

2 In a bowl, beat the egg yolks and sugar together until pale and fluffy, then gently fold in the whipped cream and vanilla essence. Whisk the egg whites in a very large, grease-free bowl until stiff, then carefully fold in the yolk mixture.

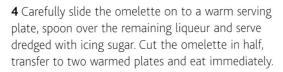

3 Melt the butter in an omelette pan. When sizzling, pour in the egg mixture and cook until set underneath, shaking the pan occasionally. Spoon on the strawberries and their liqueur and, tilting the pan, slide the omelette so that it folds over.

4 Carefully slide the omelette on to a warm serving plate, spoon over the remaining liqueur and serve dredged with icing sugar. Cut the omelette in half, transfer to two warmed plates and eat immediately.

Cook's Tip
You can give your omelette a professional look by marking sizzling lines on top. Protecting your hand with an oven glove, hold a long, wooden-handled skewer directly over a gas flame until it becomes very hot and changes colour. Sprinkle the top of the omelette with icing (confectioners') sugar, then place the hot skewer on the sugar, which will caramelize very quickly. Working quickly, before the skewer cools, make as many lines as you like.

SERVES TWO

INGREDIENTS

75g/3oz/³⁄₄ cup strawberries

45ml/3 tbsp Kirsch, brandy
   or Cointreau

3 eggs, separated

30ml/2 tbsp caster
   (superfine) sugar

45ml/3 tbsp double (heavy)
   cream, whipped

a few drops of vanilla
   essence (extract)

25g/1oz/2 tbsp butter

icing (confectioners')
   sugar, sifted

Hot Quince Soufflés

Dare to be different and keep your guests guessing about the fruit. However, if quinces are not available, substitute pears.

SERVES SIX

INGREDIENTS

2 quinces, peeled, cored
   and diced
60ml/4 tbsp water
115g/4oz/½ cup caster
   (superfine) sugar, plus
   extra for sprinkling
melted butter, for greasing
5 egg whites
icing (confectioners')
   sugar, for dusting

For the pastry cream
250ml/8fl oz/1 cup milk
1 vanilla pod (bean)
3 egg yolks
75g/3oz/⅓ cup caster
   (superfine) sugar
25g/1oz/¼ cup plain
   (all-purpose) flour
15ml/1 tbsp Poire
   William liqueur

Cook's Tip
Poire William is a clear, colourless pear eau-de-vie, which is sometimes sold with a ripe pear in the bottle. Kirsch also works well in this recipe.

1 Place the quinces in a pan with the water. Stir in half the sugar. Bring to the boil, cover and simmer for 10 minutes until tender. Remove the lid and boil until most of the liquid has evaporated. Cool slightly, then process the fruit in a blender or food processor. Press through a sieve into a bowl. Set aside.

2 Make the pastry cream. Pour the milk into a pan. Add the vanilla pod and bring to the boil over a low heat. Meanwhile, beat the egg yolks with the caster sugar and flour until smooth. Strain the hot milk on to the yolks, whisking until smooth. Discard the vanilla pod. Return the mixture to the clean pan and heat gently, stirring until thickened. Cook for 2 minutes more, whisking constantly. Remove the pan from the heat and stir in the quince purée and liqueur. Cover the surface with clear film (plastic wrap) to prevent it from forming a skin.

3 Preheat the oven to 220°C/425°F/Gas 7. Place a baking sheet in the oven to heat. Butter six 150ml/¼ pint/⅔ cup ramekins and sprinkle the insides with caster sugar. In a grease-free bowl, whisk the egg whites to stiff peaks. Gradually whisk in the remaining caster sugar, then fold the whites into the pastry cream.

4 Divide the mixture among the ramekins and level the surface. Run a knife around the side of each ramekin, then place them on the baking sheet and bake for 8–10 minutes until risen and golden. Dust with icing sugar and serve.

Hot Blackberry and Apple Soufflés

The deliciously tart, fruity flavours of blackberry and apple and the zesty taste of orange are the perfect combination. This pretty pink soufflé makes a light, mouthwatering and surprisingly low-fat hot dessert.

MAKES SIX

INGREDIENTS

butter, for greasing
150g/5oz/³⁄₄ cup caster
  (superfine) sugar, plus
  extra for dusting
350g/12oz/3 cups
  blackberries
1 large cooking apple, peeled,
  cored and finely diced
grated rind and juice of
  1 orange
3 egg whites
icing (confectioners')
  sugar, for dusting

1 Preheat the oven to 200°C/400°F/Gas 6 and put a baking sheet in it to heat. Generously grease six 150ml/¹⁄₄ pint/²⁄₃ cup soufflé dishes with butter and dust with caster sugar, shaking out any excess.

2 Cook the blackberries, apple and orange rind and juice in a pan for 10 minutes, or until the apple has pulped down well. Press through a sieve into a bowl. Stir in 50g/2oz/¹⁄₄ cup of the caster sugar. Set aside to cool, then put a spoonful of the fruit purée into each dish and smooth the surface. Set the dishes aside.

3 Whisk the egg whites in a large grease-free bowl until they form stiff peaks. Gradually whisk in the remaining caster sugar until stiff and glossy. Fold in the remaining fruit purée and spoon the mixture into the prepared dishes. Level the tops and run a table knife around the edge of each dish.

4 Place the dishes on the hot baking sheet and bake for 10–15 minutes until the soufflés have risen well and are lightly browned. Dust the tops with icing sugar and serve immediately.

dessert soufflés & omelettes

Chocolate Soufflés

These rich, individual soufflés have the merest hint of orange in them, and are divine with the white chocolate sauce poured into the middle.

1 Generously butter six 150ml/¼ pint/⅔ cup ramekins. Sprinkle each with caster sugar, shaking out any excess. Place them on a baking sheet.

2 Melt the chocolate and butter in a bowl set over a pan of simmering water, stirring. Remove from the heat and cool slightly, then beat in the egg yolks and liqueur, if using. Set aside, stirring occasionally.

3 Preheat the oven to 220°C/425°F/Gas 7. Gently whisk the egg whites until frothy. Add the cream of tartar and whisk vigorously to soft peaks. Gradually whisk in the caster sugar until stiff and glossy.

4 Stir one-third of the whites into the chocolate mixture to lighten it, then pour the mixture over the remaining whites and gently fold in. Spoon the combined mixture into the prepared dishes.

5 To make the white chocolate sauce, put the chocolate and cream into a small pan. Place over a very low heat and warm, stirring constantly until melted and smooth. Remove from the heat and stir in the liqueur and orange rind, then pour into a serving jug (pitcher) and keep warm.

6 Bake the soufflés for 10–12 minutes until risen and set, but still slightly wobbly in the centre. Dust with icing sugar and serve with the warm sauce.

SERVES SIX

INGREDIENTS

butter, for greasing
45ml/3 tbsp caster
   (superfine) sugar, plus
   extra for dusting
175g/6oz plain (semisweet)
   chocolate, chopped
150g/5oz/10 tbsp unsalted
   (sweet) butter, diced
4 large (US extra large)
   eggs, separated
30ml/2 tbsp orange
   liqueur (optional)
1.5ml/¼ tsp cream of tartar
icing (confectioners') sugar,
   for dusting

For the white
chocolate sauce
75g/3oz white
   chocolate, chopped
90ml/6 tbsp whipping cream
15–30ml/1–2 tbsp
   orange liqueur
grated rind of ½ orange

Index